good deed rain

© Copyright 2014 Allen Frost
Good Deed Rain
Bellingham, Washington
ISBN: 978-1-933964-97-3

Credits

Cover photo & design: Michael Paulus

Flower back cover photo: Allen Frost

Back cover photo of my grandmother, 1921

Illustrations: Allen Frost

Apple by TFK!

If you have enjoyed this book
please share it with someone

PLAYGROUND

Allen Frost

I've been wanting to do a new poetry book
for a while. I had a lot of chapbooks
written over the years to collect from.
At first I wasn't sure how to present them.
Then I realized, these poems needed to be
ordered in seasons, the old-fashioned
Japanese way like a haiku collection.
I don't mind this book starting slowly or
ending quietly. Hopefully you'll enjoy the circle
and even reread this, turning the wheel again.

                      Allen Frost
                      May 5, 2014
                      Bellingham, Washington

1
SPRING & SUMMER

Soft Rain

A deer
stands there
merges into green

When I get near
I almost can't see her
staring back at me

Rainy Morning

The ground sodden
walking in woods on
the loam of fir needles
breathing the sweet
cold air

The Cow Ghost

In the new woods, alder trees have sprung up
along the pond during the last thirty years.
All that's left of the dream this used to be a farm
a few posts stuck leaning in blackberry
some ragged screws of barbed wire holding
them together. Seen through the leaves
the houses built twenty years ago steam
in the morning. My dog pauses to smell
and I stop too, knowing it's near.
Close by, the ghost of a cow
hovers in the air.

The Plastic-Coated Cat

Across the wet lawn
the sound of vinyl
gives it away

The Willow Orchard, Part 1

In the early spring
I plant ten willows
across the backyard

The ground is wet
blackberry vines
birds and the rushing
river sound of I-5

The River Lover

Each shovel full of earth
fills quickly with water
that wells downhill

Be like a lover
gathering the river
mounded and adored
by your hands

Spring Ladder

Every spring
I take the ladder
from the barn
to air it out

cobwebs float
winter laundry

I climb up
green paint drops
last year's job
left on the steps

The Float

A cloud, spraining along
ten feet above the sidewalk
choosing a garden to rain upon

Stuck in the Air

If someone took
the ladder away
he would stay there
marooned
small as a sparrow
stuck in the air

On the Beautiful Planet

even the raindrops
fall without fearing
knowing where
they are going

Worm Salvage Work

Spring rain
brings them
above ground

Stranding them
on tar

There's only so much
you can do

Saving a worm
is taking a meal
from a bird

Everything Thrown Out in the Rain

Piled to the rafters of the sky
dressers and cabinets and
a mattress stacked and leaned
on boxes with broken seams
undone by morning rain
it looks like someone let
their house go out the door.
Then I slow my bicycle
even coast off the road
onto the crackling gravel
when I see the globe.
How could they throw
away the world?
I ride up to it
to give it a look.
Continents bruise
an orange ring goes
around the equator.
It wasn't cared for well
but do I have room
to carry the planet
while I pedal to work?

Basho, the Japanese Poet

He became a clerk
at the waterworks
counting waves
keeping track
in a ledger
not difficult
but his mind
began to wander
and soon after
his body followed

The Gray Street Cherries

A bus ride
another rainy day
looking outside

pink and white
flowering trees
line the road

Weather Trade

I was waiting
for a delivery
to arrive
from far away
where
they had
too much
sunshine
and were
willing to trade
a box of sun
for a bucket
full of rain

The Chestnut

Waiting all winter
at the bus stop
finally pulling
a green dress on

Silkworms

Suspended
from trees
just beginning
to blossom

Green & Yellow

Dandelions
I never noticed
have grown
on the lawn

Outside

Reading poems
I tip the page
to catch sunlight
on the words

Little Soul

Looking into
the rabbit's eyes
it hops away
before I say
hello

Neighborhood Stories

The deer
are getting
daring

watching
in windows

one goes
up the driveway
eats our flowers
hangs around
acting like
he owns the place

In Other Words

When I see deer
in the neighborhood
I give them room

I know I'm the one
dreaming in their home

Don't Forget the

flowers out there
not far from your door

Mountain Flowers

Far from sight
the mountain
pours the creek

all that way
waters flow

flowers wait
on the bank
to grow

Settled In

Dry May
weather
far from
the roaring
elevation
of the river

The stone
settles in
the garden
to endure
the quiet here

Tuned To Water

Tuned to water
this river rock
from Mt. Baker
awaits rain
or a sprinkler
even the poured
overflow run
off a flowerpot
the smallest drop
may hold
mountain
memories

No Snow This Year

Only a street
full of white
cherry blossoms
that stick
to your feet

The Rhododendron Seller

All these years later
you can tell where he was
going house to house
pulling his cart along
filled with purple flowers

The Beehive Recital

I had the rare fortune on that yellow day
to be in a field of tall grass and clover
getting closer and closer, trying to find
where that sound was coming from.
It seemed to have legs like me
it could be far away or near.
When I found it, I got close as I dared.
There in the hollow body of a tree
the drone of three hundred bees
turning their hum into honey.

Spindled Out

Caught in sunlight
unrolled silver
the steel girders
made by spiders
spindled out
on the breeze
to bridge overhead

A Glass Of Wind

In a field
overgrown
with flowers
dandelions
and daisies

A breeze
bends them
and pours them
like water

If I pick a handful
to bring home
they will need
arranging in
a glass of wind

The Curve

I found the curve
of a new world

the sun and moon
conspired with
the stars aligned

as I trace
my finger along
your skin

Sleep

Sleep to cover
calm when
we lay down
blankets drawn
off the line
in a dreaming
goodnight

The Extra Day

They were so in love
they made a prayer
for an extra day
so he could stay
and it worked
perfectly
the clock
beside her bed
couldn't move
the sun stopped
in the tree
outside her window
beyond her room
it all fell apart
the buses and trains
flower shops, factories
nobody else knew
what to do but
talk in a panic
and listen to the news
where the day played as
some sort of disaster
but for them
it was just
what they asked for

Petals

Open the shades
the sun shines
on flowers

another day
starts with
petals, colors
the miraculous
small events
unfolding

Walking with a Flower

Listening to you
I believe you too
love is all
a heart as open
as a flower
knowing
nothing else
matters

The Hidden Place

It's sort of tucked away
remove a brick and it's there
some prized treasure from childhood
kept in a piece of cloth soft as water
keepsakes that catch the light
cat's eye marbles, beach glass
an old plastic silver toy

Whistling Apricot

Whistling
while eating
this apricot
talking to
evening birds

Apricot Music

We share half
a sour apricot

This brass bell
I'm left holding

June Weather

The blanket on
the laundry line

everytime
it starts to dry

here comes
the rain

Umbrella

The umbrella
folded to the porch
stays there testing the weather

hung on the wall
with a little nest of rain
hiding inside

Library Spider

Good luck to
the library spider
with a house spun
in Literature

Knowing you're lonely
Emily Dickinson
might send a fly
to your door

Red Leaf

A red leaf
on the ground
the last day
of June

That must be
a mistake

Fall slept
in a tree
last night
painted a leaf
for practice
and dropped it
in the dew

Rhododendron

Done with blooming
the rhododendron
hands out blossoms
to the ground

Speckled Dog

Laying down
she blends
with blossoms

Lawn Mower

Mowing the yard
saving a patch
where daisies grow

Swallowtail

It's easy to imagine
that's a little person
with black and yellow
wings attached and a
lifelong love of flowers

The Bumbling Bee

Anywhere
I see a flower
attracting bees
there's me
bumbling
at beauty

The Bird Planet

It's like another planet, tall trees
shade and green, surrounded by
songs of birds I cannot see

A Family of Deer

Stopping for a family of deer
the mother leads the way
followed by two spotted babies
then the father wearing horns
who stops to glance at me
before they leave.
In just a few steps
I'm right where they were
their smell stays in the air
like the smoke of a campfire.

The Underwater Dog

When she jumped
off the dock into the lake
she sunk to a yellow blur

Underwater
it's deep and black
though she shows
standing on soft mud
eyes open
looking around

The surface had time
to settle back into
smooth reflection
clouds and trees
before she realized
she couldn't breathe
and came back up again

One Morning Instead

One morning I went in the backyard
and gathered the hippos. They were sleepy
but they followed me down the driveway
underneath the chirping branches to the sidewalk.
I know this isn't something you're supposed to do
but sometimes we do it anyway.
It was the beginning of a sunny day
and we played hippo checkers and yes
before long the traffic was stopped and
all those people who hurry around
have something new to do instead.

The Dragonfly Driver

He wears a bright yellow uniform
spins the big wooden wheel
and turns sharply in the wind.
For a while every day
the dragonfly shows up in the warm
sunshine above the field.
It's my lunch-break and I like to get
out of the office for some fresh air.
I have my spot on the bench and
a field full of dandelion slopes
down to Garden Street with trees
and a view of the harbor.
Of course I like to watch that dragonfly
and I'm sure the little driver in there
knows me by now. We share
the same world and both of us
have things to do, but doing them
can wait.

The Shepherd from Iran

He was going to watch our dog for us
but there is too much happening in his life.
He doesn't know what he's doing
or if he should be here at all.
He doesn't know what it is
right now he's going through a hard time.
These days he takes long walks
with his setar or a staff in his hand
or he just sits in his house alone.
He wonders if maybe it has
something to do with his childhood
when his country was at war.
He would sit on the rooftop and
watch the airplanes bombing.
The people would be told to hide
underground. Instead, there was
an uncle who took care of them.
He would lead the children from town
playing his guitar and singing
as they followed in a dusty line
away from the rockets and explosions
into the hills where the citrus trees
were spun with silkworm tapestries
and nobody out there knows
who you are.

DC-3 Be Gone

I was doing some gardening the day before
our vacation clipping around a patch of red cedars
when I saw a DC-3. The silver wings on it blinked.
It got so close to me it stung my elbow as it veered
back to land. I could see where it went. There were
others too, coming and going. I quickly stepped
away to a distance where I could watch safely.
They swarmed about. I had stirred them up.
As I observed them buzz angrily over the treetops,
I knew what I would have to do. You just can't have
an airport this close to your house, where you like to
garden, where your children play ball with a
zeppelin, where your wife likes to read billboards
in the sun. So I went to the store to the aisle in back.
It's amazing, there's a deterrent for every possible
pest. There were hanging sticky-strips for P-51s and
traps for Greyhound buses. If there's a freeway
running through your yard you can get rid of that
too. I found what I needed, a can of spray on the
shelf with big bold orange letters, *DC-3 Be Gone*.
I read the tiny directions. It looked okay. I bought it
and brought it home. The rest of the day I watched
out my window, waiting for the sun to fall, keeping
an eye on that spot where they flew in and out.
Those directions written so small on the can told me
to wait until well dark or early morning when the
quiet air was cool and still and the DC-3s were all
fast asleep.

Another Ferris Wheel

Formed tonight
it looks like
it chose
that spot
on Lakeway
to grow
with cars
and stars
thrown round
in a halo

The Nightbird

Listen for
the last bird
tonight

one song

time to
turn off
the light

Satori

Riding a swing
seeing over the roofs
above the everyday

catching
a rare glimpse
before returning

Going To Ohio

Since I don't know
when I'll ever get
to Europe or Asia
or far off Africa
I have to pretend
going to Ohio
will be a journey
to a marvelous land

I'll have to look
at everything
with amazement

Will I need
a guidebook
to explain
the customs
and behaviors?
Will there be
snowy mountains
beautiful moonlit seas
what stories
will inspire me?

Almost a Cardinal

Hear a cardinal
only see a red rose
shaking

Ohio Garden

A garden filled
with Ohio weeds
someone tried
a long time ago
to make it work
but what's left
from farming days
scrap metal grown
an old wheelbarrow
bowing on its wheel

Holy Water

That dew
in spider circles
little water buckets
left after rain

So holy
to get close
but I wouldn't dare
tip them all
and spill
the web

Praying Mantis

How many years
have children
been taunting
the praying mantis?
This porky kid
says it will
jump on your neck
The other says
he wants to hit
it with a rock
but there it holds
to the window screen
of the restaurant
and here am I
telling them
please be kind
look at it
it's amazing
I feel like
the old man
in a story
from Japan
where sea turtles
turn into kings

Heron Doing Time

A bird
with one wing
remembering
flying

Above the Field

trying
to get it
airborne
the way
a kite
will slide
out of hands
before catching
the wind

Sundown

sunflower
staring at
the ground

The Bed

A used-car lot
provides the bed
we pulled out from
the checkered couch

Take it
for a spin
tonight
drive it
to sleep
if you can

Green Yarn

At night
she knits
the lawns
around town
a little longer

Limpets

They live on
the roar of
the passing trains

Those houses
by the tracks
like limpets
in the surf

Out of the Plant

She told her story
on the bench
in front of Discount
All I overheard
as I walked by
"She got escorted
out of the plant"
and the man
next to her
like the radiator
to her thought
let out a sigh

Away from Work

Today is Friday!
that thought
was a shock

All it took
was a week
away from work
to forget
well ordered
days

Climate Control

Things just go on
around the weather
If there's thunder
it doesn't matter

Anymore

Trains are cutting through
all the time, that shiny scar
rail crossing is ever warm

I don't think they know
this place, this town
a blur to blow a horn
and we don't even count
those trains anymore

The Marx Birds

Reading Groucho Marx
the sound of Sunday
morning cartoon
in the other room
I finally get up
to go see…
my son watching
a girl dancing
with four birds

For Louie

Ohio afternoon
is no place
for a werewolf

He paces low
from window
to window
the carpet is hot
under his feet

Locked in the room
he clings to a dream
where he takes off
his fur and suddenly
becomes a man
selling ice cream

Playground

Found a cricket
in the grass
by the swing
tired
worn out
from music
and moonlight
all night

Lady Day

It doesn't take
a special radio
to hear music
from those days

Put a flower
in your hair
and listen to it
play

Free Kittens

Another sign
a mile from one
just like it
on Berlin Road

Around here
they grow
cats like corn
then they
draw signs
on cardboard
to give them
away

Clockwork Rabbit

The day starts
with the rabbit
in the yard

and ends
with the rabbit
there again

Ring Chimes

no string
of flowers
however beautiful
can parade with
that sound
in the wind

Lake Erie

Today
a butterfly
made its way
over Lake Erie

then turned
quickly around
remembering
the land

Welcomes

Coming into
a big city
even if
your map
directions
are wrong
the radio
welcomes
with songs

3 Elephants
In Cleveland

Today we saw
three elephants
in Cleveland

Of course
they've been there
all along

The Cleveland Monarch
Butterfly Club

You may see them
leaping off brick walls
their orange wings
turned soot gray
by cars and industry
they fly toughened
on the juice of flowers

Cleveland Block

Look up
the geese
are flying
low above
the eaves
just beyond
our reach

Laundry Chutes

Those secret canals
run echoes
through houses

I open
this one
to drop
a towel down

I stop
and hear
a radio
Billy Eckstine
carried up

Cleveland Disappears

Outside
the window
Cleveland
disappears
gradually
purples
first sirens
then crickets
then dark

Perry Como Pure Gold

The cassette tape
on a shelf upstairs
with the toothpaste
lotions and colognes
romantic reminders

A Whale

Before you go outside
hot as a furnace
remember to grab
a string beside
the door

Take a shadow
from the ocean
with you

You'll be glad
to have a whale
cool and big
casting blue
over you

The Hummingbird

I've watched
the hummingbird
arrive every day
living on flowers

I know the feeling
sped through
a garden
and gone

Salting

Salting the tree
with egrets
settling for
the night

Even If

Even if
we could stay
the reality
probably
would be
hard times
finding a job
a house
money worries
and sometimes
a loneliness
deep as water

Last Day

Last day
on Lake Erie
there are clocks
tied in trees
and the beach
runs sand
to the sea

Pictures & Words

We draw in the sand
race to finish
pictures and words
before the waves
wash in

Slow Bicycles

Slow bicycles
creak with crickets
it's so nice
to take it easy
sit in a chair
until the day
turns to shade
knowing
if you can
make it here
you've got it made

Ohio Pull

Still feeling
the weight of land
wanting to hold on
the plane lifted
off the pull of Ohio
and we are going
on the way home

Old Sights

Ohio is old
buildings
and bridges

Our sights
are mountains
and rivers

2
FALL & WINTER

Returning

Affected
by adventures
resisting the usual
run-of-the-mill
tracks and traps
that await
back at work

To Sweeten

After work
walking home
stopping
for blackberries
to sweeten
my mouth

Blackberry Family Portrait

Arranged so nobody
could pick them from
that perfect picture
framed in vines

They can't be eaten
this blackberry family
they need to be left
to grow old together

The Good Morning

I must bring
this good feeling
with me

Carried by fog
I must be going
the right way

morning bike ride
smell of the sea
on wet streets

yellow apple
I slow and tap
off the road

racing a bee
downhill
my bicycle wins

summer's end
first rain
diamonds

sitting outside
it's raining circles
on the dry bricks

after summer
the sky remembers
how to rain

The Sunny House

It was a gray day
either raining
or waiting to again
so I started the motor

The house gave a shake
and we moved
down the driveway
onto the road

Cars pulled aside
we trailed a fence
and telephone wires
driving for miles
waving out windows
leaving the old
until we arrived
in a new space
with a sunny yard

Summer Things

It's getting cold
find the last summer
things to keep you warm

Red Wagon

The red wagon
filled with dirt

pulled across
the grass

leaving
tulip bulbs
planted

Monday morning
ground mist
working the field

tilling the soil
the crows pop up
along the rows

The Eyes of Animals

Walking past
a klatch of crows
they sense
even the smallest
change in step
break in rhythm
or movement
out of ordinary

Like the snake
I saw yesterday
who froze
to blend
with leaves

They watch me
waiting to see

one crow
on top of the fir
sees more than we do

stopped like a balloon
over a little village
with mushroom roofs

fog so thick
a cat can walk
on top of it

The Foghorn
Calls For Them

The hills are gone
clouds folded down

From the harbor
the foghorn
calls them home

A Code

A code
in the day
to day goes
unbroken
by most

But I
can feel it
all around me

Every day
I go out
knowing
the world
is big enough
to get lost in

Barns

There's nothing like finding yourself
lost in fog and a spinning clock
on a road serenaded by cows
in a hundred clouds
shoals of barns
all alike in the night

Cow

I live in green
I eat flowers
I stand around
watching the clouds
or watching the ground

Blackberry Player Piano

I rolled the piano
on wooden skids
like the Egyptians did
with their pyramids

Up the backyard hill
deep in the crushed weeds
the wheels finally tangled
beneath the apple tree

I know how it works
feed blackberry vines
into the player piano
so it reads the thorns
as notes

Every pull
out of the ground
you can hear
a different song

raking leaves
and fallen plums
all wet together

put down the rake
is there time to show
the hiding garden snake

Chestnut Tree

Wilted with the weight
of the summer's end
that chestnut works
to drop its leaves

The Fall Car

Parked
under the tree
the black car
waits for
an apple
to fall

Bird Shaped Leaf

Your flight
took you
to the ground

Varied Thrush

The dead bird
beside the road
folded in periwinkle
eyes turned off
already flown to
the next destination

Clouds Surround
an Orange Moon

In the path ahead
a deer sees me
lit by rain
hooves clatter
on the bridge
above the creek

Ray

Each drop
of rain
contains

salmon
cedars
Douglas firs

The Good Couch

A tipped couch
in a creek

what good
does it bring
those downstream

will it taint
their water plaid
with soft pollution

or will the faint
sound pouring
through its cloth
bring comfort
to the tired

and finally
eventually
will it fade
with civilization
as water wears
everything away

Cold Wet Dog

Open the door
to cold wind
rain and fur

Summer is Gone

Let the dog out
she just stands there
smelling the air

Umbrella Story

Followed by a moth
looking for shelter
in these black eaves
I hold to the rain

Love Again

Stand in
the rain
and the roses

Hold hands
again

Remember
who we are

I Have Imagined
And Now We Are Real

You are in a little boat
my hands are about you
then I put them to water
and we row upon our dreams

My heart rides a cloud
We have found each other
I love you
I have imagined
and now we are real

19th Century Bird

Early bird up
in the ashes
pulling thread
from our sleep

Sing for the light
let morning grow

Go when the sun
gets bright

The Panda Bears

The panda bears
have done it again
leaving the woods
a reminder
leaves pulled
in a wet circle
branches tossed
and bent over
their bed

Thursday Morning

A deer beside
the swimming pool

morning sky
reflected on water

The Word Tree

The word tree
drops its leaves
every October
crumpled letters
scatter the streets

Only

I walk on
red leaves

The trees
shut down
for winter

Only scratches
standing there
waiting shapes
above me

This Hand

This hand
holds
another hand
I cannot see

I know
you know me
though we
are far away

Halo

I have
a prayer
I haven't said

I keep it
whirling
overhead

Waiting for Sleep

The cuckoo clock
in their house
would go off
every half hour

Even now
I can hear
that little
wooden bird

At 2 A.M

A goose
goes over
the house
waking me
with a horn

The Highway Surf

Awake before
the alarm clock
I listen to cars

Walking the Dog Story

It was a rainy morning and still black as night
as he took his dog outside for a walk. He stopped
at the shoulder of the road to put a hand over his dog
while a big truck growled by close. When it was gone
he pointed and they were off. The dog's white tip tail
made it easy to keep track of as it stopped at places
along the way. They caught up with a sidewalk
and the man took that path. They passed around
three highschool students wearing Halloween
costumes. Then it got quiet. It was just his dog and
him…rain, his shoes, the click of the dog's collar.
Each morning he took his dog out before he left
for work. Summer had been nice, but now it was
getting cold and wet. They were about to turn
around back home when he stopped. He stared
down a long street he had never seen before.
Overnight it had just appeared. It went downhill
with tall old-looking streetlamps to light the way.
He took a step then his dog led. Whispering under
their feet were hundreds of yellow shining leaves,

bright as gold.

Video

One cold autumn day
he walked up the broken
pathway to our door
He had a box of videos
for sale. He said
"I'm living in my car."
So we bought *Fantasia*
and wished him well
and away he went
crunching every leaf
he landed on.

The Wishing Well Custodian

Money loses
meaning here

Coins are cold
to the touch

What matters
is cleaning
sweeping wishes
into a pan

Big Ideas

He brought home
an old motorcycle
a year ago

It hasn't moved
from the lean
on the fence

Big ideas
get quiet
when left alone

Everything Is
Going Somewhere

Cat on
the riverbank
watching leaves

the same wind
pushing me

Mr. & Mrs. Soft and Warm

A little rabbit crackles in the leaves next to the path.
At first I think what a frozen morning for you to be
out then I realize, I'm the one walking in the cold
to a job all day. He's going down a lantern-lit hall
into the warm earth to lay in a nest with a wife
all murmured in fur.

Walking in the Snow

stopping to hear
the dead silence
hanging in the air

Pink Mountain

Pink light
on the mountain

The moment I turn
to tell someone

it's gone

Winter Apples

Like light bulbs
picked from
bare branches
carried over
crunching snow
brought home
poured into
a wooden bowl
Winter apples
fill our room
with a red
and yellow
glow

Porcelain

We stayed inside to watch
small refrigerators falling
from a white sky

A Loom in the Snow

Last night with Rustle tucked into bed
he asked me about Emily Dickinson
I recited one of her poems and said
how her words always have
that rhythm that's all her own
as if some New England steam-driven
sled is gliding past us on the snow

The 5 Year Old Land

There are years
where they believe
anything you say
fairy tales
talking animals
everything is real
Growing older
that doesn't leave
it just goes
to another place
Suspended
on a thin line
pulled out far
to the clouds
like a balloon
you still hold to

2:50 A.M.

I can't sleep
when the house
pops and creaks
in the wind

Song of the Tin Man

She woke him up because she heard music.
"It's jazz," she said. "It's the roaring twenties."
The Tin Man got out of bed miserably and
clanked to the stairway. He stood there listening.
He even took off his funnel cap to listen through.
Silence. So he went back to the bedroom.
"I don't hear anything."
"You don't hear jazz?"
"Nope." He got back under the covers.
Four hours later they were awakened at dawn
by the music on the clock radio alarm.

The Creature

What is that
ghostly creature
moving up the road

it slows
it stops
it sees me

now I know
this animal
is not from here

all it can do
is wander

another ghost
in the air

I wonder
how many
go about us
each day

The Sawhorse

She has the ability
propping four legs
to hold her up

In the kitchen
anywhere you turn
you have to step
around our dog

Bus Sound

Laying in bed
a bus goes by
I know that sound
I could be on it
going somewhere

Unwinding

Not like the wind
the way you live
belongs to the clock
not the natural way
when the pace of a day
goes unwinding in the leaves

Some Days

Sometimes
it feels
I'm standing
in the tide

Some days
the waves
knock me
down

Winter Trees

Black capped chickadees
so small their call could be
coming from the trees

Watching Crows

from the top of the hill
they hold wings out
following the air
folding down
all that distance
to the shore

The Hula Hoop Hero

The house on 25th Street with the hula hoop stuck
high in the bare winter branches bothered him.
Finally he took a ladder to their yard, set it under
the pink hoop and took it down. Back on the ground
he carried it and leaned it against their door.
At first he felt like the Lone Ranger, some unknown
hero who did a good deed then slipped away. But
as he stood there ready to turn into the cold dawn
and leave, he suddenly had a troubling thought,
What if they *wanted* it in the tree? It could be their
anchor. What if their world clung to the fact that it
was there? He didn't know anymore. Paused on their
doorstep, mind spinning it over, he reached wearily,
clutched the plastic tubing and carried it back to
the tree. Up the silver rungs to the same height as
before, he hung it on that branch in its place again
like a lantern out of reach of ordinary humans.

Directions Folded to a Bird's Wing

Walk down the steep hill, on a sidewalk
split by the roots of trees arching overhead.
Turn the corner to the left and then
you can hear the birds. It's an aviary attached
to a house like a screened porch trying hard
to bring the sky down and cage it in a space
only ten feet by ten. I've seen this through all
the seasons. In the gray wet Seattle winter
it's covered by plastic so the cold can't get in.
Rather than that, I'll remember it as summer
when those African finches are singing their
hearts out and the sparrows and even the crows
will come to the bent wire corners to listen.

Spent Time

Spent time
under wing
sheltering
protected from
the elements
watched over
cared for
sung to
and let go

3
SPRING & SUMMER

Morning, Bus Stop

Dandelions
grown by the moon
a frog croaking all alone

Under Water on the Lawn

I've been wanting to say something about that boat
for a long time, noticing these American ghosts that
reappear in strange places. On a shoal of dandelions
sitting in the rain, the hull was caged in the yard for
ages. It was only the fiberglass shell hollowed out.
The lawn grew around it and whatever washed
alongside, sometimes toys depending on the people
who were renting the house. Then one day
someone finally spraypainted PT-109 on the bow
facing the street. From the sunken world war
depths of a coral sea it was resurrected and
rechristened for this green unmown lawn in
Washington. Naming it gave it some notoriety,
it was a local landmark. Once I was stopped
in the woods by someone with a heavy backpack
asking for directions to it. But like its earlier
incarnation, it was doomed to a short life.
The sides collapsed in the weather softened
like wax by the rainy seasons and at last
the boat was torn apart and carted away.
After a while the yellow shadow of it left in
the grass regrew. Time goes on, the house
rents out, different cars park on that edge
of yard still haunted by the legacy of Kennedy.

International Orange

Day 1:
I started building the Golden Gate Bridge
last night, laying down cardboard in seven foot
lengths on the cement floor of the barn,
two towers to be constructed from five
overlapping pieces. The first day ends with
ten planks resting against the green wall
in the living room.

Day 2:
I'm picturing those tall red towers.
In my mind there's a blueprint spread out,
paper the color of San Francisco bay.
I carry the plans, they float wherever I go.
I want to spend another day thinking about it.

Day 3:
A fog crept in, I'm tired. That was a long
nine hours at work and biking home in
the rain, too worn-out to work anymore.
Anything that might have happened didn't.
No bridge building, only the mutter of
outboard motors circling unseen.

Day 4:
Yes, this morning I stand in the rain
under a white sky full of gulls
and I notice the fog poured over
Chuckanut Hills. It's a sign
from San Francisco.

Day 5:
Last night I cut the sections for one tower
and started on the other. Today, I sat
in the sun at lunch and read about
the poets of San Francisco.
Finished the second tower using
the first one as a template to trace.

Day 6:
I try to press the tower sections
together using a hot glue gun.
It dries too fast and won't hold.
Remember the red bolts in 1935
flung and tightened into place,
clapping iron to iron. Tomorrow
I'll get some brass fasteners.
It will look more authentic too
with the cardboard riveted.

Day 7:
Work comes to a halt. Not because of
weather conditions, the tides, or workers
on strike. I went out and brought home
a little plastic box of 100 brass fasteners,
¾" long. Only used eight. Need longer ones
to hold the bridge together. Oh well.
That will happen tomorrow.

Day 8:
Painted it a burnt orange, the closest
match I could find to the real color,
International Orange. Thick yarn for
the cables connecting the towers.

Day 9:
The Golden Gate Bridge
stands beside a big window,
with a view down Cedar Street,
to ocean water shrouded over
with March fog. The scene is complete.
The only thing it could use, I suppose,
a cardboard crowd to march across,
some sun, and the 37th latitude.

March Morning

Cold air
like a depth of sea
breathing in
I can taste
the cherry trees
blossoming

A Broom

A crow
carrying
one stick
to sweep
the tree

Two Rabbits

so small
they could fit
in my pockets

Two Spiders

He plays her
a song on
one string

approaching

She's got
all arms
waving

A Cranefly

in this clearing
carrying sunlight
on its wings

The Willow Orchard, Part 2

Four years later
only two willows
survive

You never know
what will grow
even this orchard
is proof of that

Sending Out Thoughts

My dog and I were walking in the wet woods.
The trail was rained on and the slugs were here
and there. At first I was watching out for them
so I wouldn't step on them, then it became clear
I didn't have to worry. Somehow my pace
didn't need to be altered or redirected.
No matter where they were, I missed them.
Whenever I neared, my foot would be up
in the air or land beside as if guided that way.
My dog too, trotting at my side, passed them by
every slug a lighthouse of subtle mind control
as we walked to the end of the muddy path
and back without harming a single one.

Early Summer Swallow

Small dot
on the wire
sitting alone

By the time
we find binoculars
the bird has flown

A Bird Shaped Kite

Usually I see them on a post by the highway
when I'm driving to Seattle or on some road
in Ohio. Today we were in the backyard.
Interstate-5 is our neighbor. Thousands of cars
go by day and night. We were playing tag.
I was IT so I had a little time to wander,
pretending strategy while the kids shrieked
and dodged about. On top of the hill, cars
were rushing past, I could see their roofs
through the trees. Then a hawk moved overhead
like a diamond cut piece of cardboard or a bird
shaped kite. It flew slowly downstream over cars.
Sometimes the traffic flushed out an animal for it,
that's how they hunt. It's easy to imagine that
road as glass and steel water flowing from
Canada to Mexico. I've thought of it that way
since we moved in. Like anyone else who lives
along this road, we stay because we have
adapted to changes in the natural world,
playing tag on the banks of a mechanical river.

Mermaid Laundry

When it rained
or looked like fog
rolling off the sea
she would hang her laundry
to soak on lines in the yard

Add Water

She just added water
and her house would grow.
A bucket from the faucet
and up went another story,
rooms appeared like crops in rows
as the house leaned out over power lines
forming turrets and towers past the trees.
Never happier, she slept peacefully
in a bed on the 71st floor
when the rain began to fall.
She woke up to the weather
listening to that patter on the roof.
The house shuddered all over expanding
everywhere, inflating. She ran and stared down
the long hallway growing doors into distance
like a train pulling faster and faster away
reaching rivers, estuaries, the sea
filling all of America up.

April Dream

Silver fishing boats
creaking along against
the house windows
one of the boats
with an orca whale
painted on the hull
going by the chimney
tipping it, moving by

Woken By

a coyote
across the street
when it seems
to be gone
I fall asleep

All the Puddlefish

For too long he had been collecting puddles,
keeping them in shoeboxes or envelopes,
jars, plastic bags, whatever they fit in.
With careful handwriting and attention
to detail, he had labeled each puddle
by origin and date of capture.
After years, he just had too many.
When he knew it was time, he stacked
all of them inside a wheelbarrow and
pushed it down the street into the woods.
One by one he let each one go into the creek
like fish that have spent their lives on a journey
that leads them finally to the sea.

The Lotus Pond

In front of someone's house, there are orange
goldfish in bags of water all across the yard.
The sun is warming them, some are dying,
some are dead already. What can he do about it?
Dreams may be designs in the mind or a test, but
I am not king of that world. I ride in them like
reality, when something bad happens I struggle
to get out. I watch myself in them...If only he had
the sense to make a big pond appear, lily pads,
flowering lotus, then he could set them free...
While I think about it in this morning with the
singing birds, it occurs to me—Who laid down my
dream world? Haven't I created it with those years
I've been alive? I'm sure I could draw a map of it,
it's like the opening pages in a book of Oz. I know
where there's water and forest, cities and mountains.
Why not add a pond? I can picture it there.
Thinking about it while I'm getting ready to go to
work at 6 A.M, I wonder if I've made the lotus pond
appear there and if those goldfish have found their
way.

Mr. Thank You's Cloud

We were watching *Mr. Thank You*
a 1936 film by Hiroshi Shimizu
when a Japanese cloud
in the black and white sky
flew out of our TV into our room
Nobody missed it in the movie
The bus driver was busy
standing in the tall weeds
throwing stones
down a ravine
Up, the cloud went
and stopped, curled
in the ceiling corner
next to our paper lantern
It's been there all evening
like a sleeping pillow case

Sunday Nap

Open window
green curtains
if I close my eyes
I will fall asleep

The Plum Map

The two of them
on bicycles
riding the neighborhood
knowing every tree
going to the ones
with plums

even so much later
this time of year
has a taste
a memory
to be picked
ripe from the air

Shortcut

A way
we know
goes between
concrete walls
cutting through yards
climbing wooden fences
between the leaves
narrows
in weeds
and shadows

Knowing the secret
we save time
like summer sunlight
kept in a jar
with a raindrop

Paul

Paul reminds me
to see the miraculous
to go each morning
trespassing
looking for beauty

Daisies

Thanks for growing
along the road
even among things
people throw away

Breasts

In the bathroom
at the bowling alley
a drawing of breasts
and someone has added
Do Something With Your Wife

Parking Lot Bouquet

Sunday morning
we ride bikes
around the big
square of tar
five raindrops
spitbugs and bees
we are busy
gathering flowers
enough to fill
a jar

Quiet

After the lawnmower
dies next door
you could walk
on that silence
like a deep lush field
grown in the air

Larry

Writing poems
about the Buddha
and Zen in some
little Ohio town
errands to do
the car parked
on hot tar

Rain

June rain
a robin
flies in front
flowers bent
bloom wet

Bugs

In the garden
pulling out weeds
be careful moving
in their metropolis

Dave

All that lettuce
you gave us
from your garden
delicious
green memory

Breeze

Something
comforting
stirs the air

Telephone Poles

The whole town
all our houses
connected by strings
knitted and pulled
from a ball of wire

Mt. Baker

Downtown
you hide behind
a billboard
a jumble of rooftops
a tall cottonwood
shimmering leaves

The Tooth Fairy

Get dressed
drive the car
to the grocery store
the only place open
at this late hour
so in the morning
our son will reach
under his pillow
excited to find
an avocado

Paint

A new day
street painted
by the early rain
the smell of sea
and wet leaves

Prayer

The words
you've been saying
all your life
to the world

Jason's Barn

It has fallen
like an elephant
to its knees
tiredness
the weight of paint
the years of holding
itself together
have sunk it
to the level of the
new growing corn

Nooksack River

The water carried
from the mountain
in green buckets

left in the sand
along the banks
bright specks of gold

32nd Street

Bicycles, cars
voices and flowers
we live beside
a movie
the curb
the sidewalk
our house
on the shore

Bird Taxi

At 4 AM I heard the birds at the end of our street.
Almost an hour later, I heard a car motor arrive
a door opened and the birds started in our yard.
I was too tired to get up and look out the window
so I let myself see it another way. I pictured
the yellow shiny door of a checkered cab open.
With the sound of pouring water, all those birds
from down the street flew out and found places
in our trees. A new day was beginning
they were making the rounds, singing
their hearts out. So thick you could walk
on the sound, or float on it, let your mattress
drift like a raft if it wasn't 6 o'clock and
time to get up.

Bird Taxi Purr

I woke moments before
and waited for the Bird Taxi purr
as it rubbed up to the curb and stopped.
Then it happened like it did the day before
one bird began and a few more joined in
as musicians do when meeting each other
out of the blue.

Bird Taxi Mystery

The bird orchestra was in full swing
as I heard the taxi door open and the
wet slap of something hitting cement.
The door closed and the car rolled on.
Of course I knew what it was, it wasn't
such a mystery. The taxi was an ordinary car
driven by a man who carried his family along.
When he stopped, his oldest son,
maybe seven years old, would get out
and leave a newspaper for the birds.

Bird Taxi Times

The paper is thin and crackles at
the touch. It is covered with little
scratched marks like a musical score.
This is what gets delivered early
each day so the birds can read it
and know what to say.

Bird Taxi Boy

One of these mornings, maybe tomorrow
I'll be able to lean out of bed to push
that green cloth curtain aside. Usually
I'm so tired when I hear that car I can't
move. Next time will be different though.
Yes, I will see it there, with family inside,
and the boy will leap out. Because it's
so early, the mind is thick and cloudy
the door to dreamland is wavering open.
I will watch him move up the driveway
only his feet don't touch the gravel, he is
hovering, flying actually. He drops a
newspaper near our house then he spins
and floats back to the waiting car.
The engine will carry them away.
I will let go of the curtain and it
will cover the window once more
and when I wake at a minute to six,
will I even remember what I saw?

Bird Taxi Rain

On a cold raining morning
the birds hide in leaves
tight to trees and eaves
and there's no sound at 4 AM.
My alarm clicks on at 6 AM
a muffled song that could be
anything.

Bird Taxi Bicycle

Because we're having trouble with our car
thirty years of roads and sometimes it won't go
I hope they're not in the same boat. If their car
broke down, someone would have to deliver
by bicycle, carrying the papers in bird cages
slung like lanterns roped to the frame.
Would I even hear it arrive? Only the rusted
pull of chain, pedal and creak as it went by.

Bird Taxi East

And when it passes our house, where does
it go next? The dawn isn't done, it rattles
down to the shore and the bicycle wheels
churn it west across the sea. It rises on
the east coast of Japan, and with the new
sunlight again finds a house like ours
wakens with birds and different words.

Bird Taxi Me

That could be, it's possible there is more than one me hearing birds this way. After Japan across more water to China, India, climbing Himalayas with the sun it goes. Sometimes a car sometimes it's a bike, whatever form it takes moving around the world, returning in a circle each morning to me.

Bird Taxi Belief

This spring I thought the birds that wake us arrive by taxi cab. It happens at dawn like an ordinary newspaper delivery. I have never seen it. Only because of my first impression do I keep calling the sound a taxi, and only because
I like the story, do I believe it might be true.

Today

Today I was
walking the dog
and she turned
into a cow
nuzzling leaves

Park

If you take a left
on Indian Street
look quick

there's a park

down that alley
almost invisible
like a green door
between the buildings

The Forgetting Birds

The birds
have forgotten
their words
now only
tunes remain
they sit on
branches and hum

The Silkworm

Something drifting
floating on the air
you can't quite
focus on
barely even there

Furniture in the Woods

Seeing us near
the deer bounced away
like a rocking chair

A Plastic Chair

Set a plastic chair
beside the water
anytime you want
to watch the river

P'ang Yun

Methodically
he took every item
beginning with the large
beds and couches
bookshelves, the stove
bringing them one by one
to the river's edge
It took all day
to empty his house
and not long at all
to toss everything in
When he was done
he was empty as a cup
and the water ran
over and around
what he used to be

Landmark

Every summer he would take a day off work
and drive the three of them to the berry farm.
"There's your ride out of here," he would say.
It was a yellow biplane crop-duster, lopsided
with age and disrepair so that its wings hung
into the weeds like a wet paper bird.
He would steer past and listen to his children
laugh and this went on for years. The joke
actually got better as time passed
for every year the plane looked a little
worse off, with more falling from it
and holes showing through. The plane
was sort of a landmark, just down the road
from where they would park at the farm
and spend a few hours filling cardboard flats
with ripe blueberries and raspberries and
strawberries too if the season was good.
It's funny that in all those years they
never approached the crop-duster.
The plane wasn't that far from the road.
On any one of those warm summer days
they could have left the car and walked
over to it. It would have made a good
photograph to see the kids finally posed
beside that comical airplane, hands and
shirts berry-stained from a day in the sun
ready to climb aboard a thing so fragile
the wind could be heard sighing
through the wings.

A Borrowed Bird

She had the funniest
look of disbelief
squinting through
thick glasses perched
on her nose, her mouth
open and crooked.
We must have been
over Colorado mountains
Oklahoma, or some
state in the plains
where the air can
boil up thick
in black thunder.
The turbulence
shaking our plane
got her hands gripping
the armrests.
Another spell of
bad weather hit
so I told her a story.
I know a third grader
knows better
what I was saying
was magic, made-up
on the edge of
what she knew
and what can't be.
Just there, balanced
in a neverland where
it might be true.
I explained
"Every once in a while
the big bird we're in

needs to flap its wings."
She still wasn't so sure
and maybe I should have
been more honest about it.
"Think of us going round
and round over oceans
and land in a borrowed bird.
The captain and crew
sit in the wind in front
in a crown of blinking lights
soothing the bird with buttons
and levers while we all sit
and wait in the narrow aisle
like Pinocchio in the whale.
It's a little scary I know
no wonder, think of the size
this animal traveling
like swimming in the air.
Don't worry though.
While the world spins
underneath us, those big
silver wings take us safely
where we want to go."

Pearl Street

Lawn cut down
to the quick
the chicory
purple flowers
just poking through
like periscopes
daring to grow

Paperback Crop

A room has been cleared
in the back of the house.
Everything that was in there
has been boxed and pulled out
and trucked about town
finding new homes or
I guess going into the ground.
I was handed a paperback
Tortilla Flat by Steinbeck.
This is the hot afternoon
I start to read the yellow pages
moving crisp as leaves of corn.

Tomatoes for Sale

The road goes beside
the tall green monster
wall of Genetic corn
This is the part
I can't understand
How could this fertile land
put up with that?
Where's the rebellion
the fight against
what is wrong?
That's why
it's a victory
to see a painted sign
on the chair in front
of their house
Up the dirt driveway
I can see tomatoes
growing from buckets
in their garden

Humpty Dumpty

He almost fooled me
laughing that way
on top of the wall
one arm dropped
over my shoulder
his wheezy breath
and cough at
the end of it

Franklin Construction

A red and white
dumper truck
tipped up
so it pours
a spill of walnuts

Who Wouldn't Want
A Gorilla Mask?

One warm summer evening in Ohio
I was at Goodwill and saw a gorilla mask.
I didn't have any money on me
I was wearing a tourist costume
shorts and a t-shirt
but I thought I could return
in the morning to buy it.
So I stepped back into the crickets
and twilight, thinking of all the things
I could do with that gorilla mask.
It never occurred to me there was
someone else, someone with $5
entering the store at that moment.
As I was crossing the wide parking lot
walking in the weeds next to the road
someone was pulling that mask down
off the wall and holding it like a flower.

The Ohio Window

When I open
the Ohio window
all of a sudden

this is
the cricket song
my radio
won't get
where I
come from

everyone
is in on it
the train
here and gone
the dog
that dots
with barks

I understand
a car rush
fading
like wind

inspiration
in listening

a night
like this
goes right
into dreaming

Two Cantaloupes

Seen from a distance it couldn't be what
it looked like. We drove up close to make sure
it wasn't a mirage. Two cantaloupes were left
alone on a curb in the empty parking lot.
What a strange thing to do. Or is it?
Maybe this is how Johnny Appleseed
started out. Only now it's two cantaloupes
planted in a modern meadow of tar.

The first morning chore
Ann waters the flowers
from the full rainbarrel

On A River In Ohio

We unloaded the couch
into the Vermillion River
and took it for a ride.
It's summertime
everyone is friendly
and wave to us going by.
A leisurely comfortable glide
carried along the mossy
glassy surface
rippled sometimes
by the fish below.
Swallows dipped
and threaded
and we spotted their nests
when we went under
the railroad bridge
counting the mud daubed
into the trestles.
Our chair turned
when it wanted to
presenting us with views
like a barge loaded with
flinty chips of ore,
a blue cartoon tug tied to it,
a big willow draped hushing
leaves and shadow,
crowds of boats along the bank,
houses standing like dominoes
yellow windows going on
and deep in a clutch of woods
some twilight fireflies began.
When the slow green poured
out into Lake Erie

you could tell the day
was getting done.
We came to rest
against the breakwater
blocks of rocks run aground.
Pushing aside cattails
and dark tall purple flowers
we rose to the top of stones
just in time to see the red
ball of the sun at rest
on the waves
filled with the warm
summer Ohio air going down

Satch

Satch took a correspondence course
in a little office room above the street.
He learned the different ways to fill a page.
As an exercise, the class wrote letters
to far away. At first his words to Tennessee
were formal and awkward, cold to read
as a blueprint, but somewhere along the way
he became an architect and something lonely
in him bloomed. He found he had a gift.
Something started to happen. One day
he stared deeply at certain words she wrote.
When he got her letters he took them upstairs.
He took his shoes off and lay down on the bed.
When he opened the envelope so carefully
he would pull out her folded letter and
bring it to his face, eyes closed
acting like someone in love.
Handwritten letters were precious.
He traced her motion in the air
trying to conjure her there.
He bought a record that mentioned
Tennessee. He thought of wildflowers
and green hills, he thought of her
all the time. Once he talked to
a truck driver for half an hour.
Anyone who had been there
had been that much closer than him.
She sent him her photograph and
finally, he decided he couldn't wait,
he wrote he was on his way.
He got a train ticket
arranged time off from work.
He had never felt such excitement.

It must be the warmth of Spring.
At the department store
he bought a blue suit
a pair of leather shoes
and a diamond ring.
He was floating on air
without a care to what
the suspicious world might say.
That's when it always happens.
It used to be called a Dear John letter.
On the very day he was due to leave,
there it was, typed, a text book example
it was like Day 1 all over again
an impersonal letter from Tennessee.
He read it and had to throw it away.
He went up to his bedroom
and came back down the stairs
in his socks and went to the basement.
Lit only by the last green of daylight
he found the corner by the furnace.
He set his new shoes flat
on top of the suitcase
and pushed it all the way back.
There were canning jars
berries cobwebbed in dust
time would cover it all.
With a broken fairy tale heart
he never really got over her
not even after all those years
when his shoes were brought down
the laces were brittle and the suitcase
cracked open to reveal a blue
pressed suit with crushed flowers.

Two Mourning Doves

One is sitting
on the wire
another arrives
whirring wings

It's evening
they could fly
anyplace
but this
is where
they stay

The Ohio Wheel

At night
the crickets
creak
like a carrousel

Hydrangea Legs

Two flowers
in a glass jar
their green stems
reach through water
ready to walk

Marlene Dietrich

I wonder
if anyone
still listens
to the radio
in this age

It seems
old fashioned
and gone
until I am
proven wrong

In the car
on the way
to Akron
I press
the button
and hear
her song

After a Dream

It takes a while
to get used to
this place again
Like a train
the dreamworld
clatters away
stranding me
at this station
to go start
another day

A House in Maine

Steps painted
white as snow
stacked against
the wooden house
walking up
to a door

Red Rose

This thinly made
tea cup decorated
with flowers
filled with leaves

Cuba

Opening her eyes
getting used to
the birds and flowers
warm enough to wear
a dress to the shore
where the pilot boat
waits at the harbor

Among the people
on the docks
someone plays
a big guitar
someone gives her
orchids woven fresh
into a necklace
Hello again
to friends
she hasn't seen
for seventy years

A motor starts
a ghostly plume
beside the pier
she knows the sound
down the ramp
to a little boat
painted blue
the pilot
rings a bell
and off they go

Up in the bow
the wind will be

blowing her dress
she will hold
the wooden rail
across the water
she will see him
in a steamship
getting closer
on the flying bridge
waving back to her

Gene's Beagle

Tied to the boat
hauled from the shore
he lets out a howl
whenever you show

The Lobster Wars

Coffins do not sail
in these coves anymore
laying down their lines
and buoys like territories
the boundaries of wars
fought over on water

Those days are gone
they have grown old
the last of them
living with memory
and the cold

The Blue Path

Low tides
we gathered
mussel shells
scattered them
along the path
from the sea

The Biggest Fish

My second day on the Atlantic
I tried casting and reeling
catching my limit of eelgrass
seaweed and tangled line
when along paddled a man
in a red life jacket.
"How's the fishing?" he asked.
I held up the empty bucket.
At least he was doing alright
it was a good day for swimming.
He pointed across Harpswell Sound
a thousand yards to the other side
where the Bailey Island bridge
underwent repairs. He was
the crane operator, done for today
and he was swimming home.
Hungry, tired, at the mercy of current
and tide, he was the biggest fish
I didn't catch.

Watermelon Fishing

A green watermelon
beside the sink
in the kitchen

My grandmother
cut it carefully
with the knife
used to open
so many fish
like letters
from the sea

We watched her
prepare each bite
for the mackerel
flounder and cod
red squares
she would freeze
for fishing tomorrow
hooked to a line
trolled out behind
the wooden boat
pulled through
deep green water
the irresistible lure
of summer on land

The Luna Moth

It thumped
mitten wings
on the window

Rachel's House

Long ago
I was there
in the kitchen
I remember
her telling me
in unfrightened
detail about
the ghost

I think of her
whenever
I pass that house
sitting on a fold
beside the road
where she is the ghost
who lives there now

A Yard Sale

At the fire station
I read the sign
pinned to a couch
LBJ Sat Here

Short Wave Radio

A rusted box
full of hum
and orange light
bringing him
the world
at night

Summer Reading

Pirates or volcanoes
comic book heroes
and submarines
quiet afternoons
in old houses
with green
coming in
screen windows

King Medicine

I suppose it turned into a bit of a story after all,
going to Bangor to see the Stephen King house.
It's one of those things I had to do,
even though it bothered me to. If I was in
Memphis, Tennessee I would feel the same way
about Graceland. I would have to go.
I would stand in front of that metal gate
just like the tourists do. First we stopped at
the Brunswick library to get a book on CD.
I chose *Cell* because I knew the way it just
ripped right into story. Pulling out we passed
a man in a pink shirt, smoking a pipe and
I threatened to take him along with us.
295 North was a good drive, like a painting,
calm smooth new black tar, little traffic, low pines
on either side. Caution Moose signs and after a
long while listening to *Cell* and my daughter's
occasional gasps, the garbage hill before Bangor.
It looks like a weird mountain the road bends for
and misses. Of course I thought of the drafts
that might be in there. We took Exit 184
and waited to go right on Union Street.
A beefy man with a Boston Red Sox t-shirt
crossed the walk. We passed Mansfield Stadium
a little later and saw the stands full, I thought
he's probably there. We missed West Broadway
and I had to turn onto Pond, then Cedar and
suddenly I felt we were very near.
I knew it was a red house. I saw it.
Well, it was easy to feel like a fool now
but I had to do it. The street was eighty feet
wide, mansions on either side and nobody
was parked near. I pulled over just past

the property corner with a big green frog statue.
I don't know what I expected to happen—no,
I do—I can tell it in awful truthfulness.
Like any other fan drawn here, I expected
there to be a chance of this happening:
at just this moment, he would be coming out,
a wave, I could say hello and talk a minute.
Grandpa made a call on the cell-phone
to tell where we were and shambled
at Rosa like a zombie along the curb.
We got our pictures taken awkwardly.
All the windows looked still and
I couldn't blame them. I could hear shrieks
from the baseball field a couple blocks away.
We got back in the car, but I wasn't done yet.
I had to try the stadium. I could picture him
there in the bleachers watching the game.
What a bizarre ride. The potbellied man
on the corner of Hammond wearing shorts,
black socks, an umbrella tucked under his arm.
All day long a fog had clung to the trees.
The radio kept warning about a hurricane.
He was prepared. Past the Dead River Company,
we circled those streets back onto 13th and then
we were there, I pulled off of the road.
I parked on the grass like the other cars
but I was the only one who dared to get out.
"But look," I said. I pointed to a man
on the other side of the mesh wire fence.
He sat at a picnic table, writing something.
"That might be him, right there."
When I got closer, walking past all the rows
of parked cars, I could tell it wasn't him.
The announcer inside set up another batter,
a strange sounding name, people clapped

in the tall stands. I went around to the gate
and read Senior World Series and admission
cost, 10 dollars. That stopped me. I turned
around. I went back to the car. Now
I just wanted to get a postcard to send.
I don't need to say how I even failed at that,
the Family Dollar store didn't have any,
the grocery no, nor the gas station where
there was a dwarf in front of me in line.
"I'm sorry dear," the cashier said.
It's a winding and steep river town,
old buildings, iron, stone, wooden,
people living in a dream. We saw
the Paul Bunyan statue, giant maniac
face that I've read about. I didn't really
expect to write this, I didn't take notes
the way I should have. We drove out of there,
over the Penobscot again, heading south
on Route 1, caught in tourist traffic,
a taste of my own medicine, slowed
to a crawl for every tourist town
from then on, Camden, Rockport,
Waldoboro, Damariscotta, Moody's Diner,
Wiscasset on down.

Noah Road

His path to the sea
took him past the house
with the barking dog

He could understand
that kind of urgency
the dog only wanted
to be taken along

He had a wooden boat
overturned on the sand
the oars were stored
like candlesticks inside

Seagull

With one lobster trap
set in the stern
he rowed slow
and didn't mind
the seagull
in the bow
I'm sure
he had a name
for the bird
but we didn't
stop to ask

Tree Cup

From the beginning
it was a tea bag
I dug into ground
patted it over
with the toe
of my shoe
and then
after all these years
here I am again
I have to reach
up to a branch
where the ripe
teacup is waiting

Alice on the Seashore

She follows a gull
over the seaweed
stones capped
with barnacles

Lighthouse

The storm is gone
ocean calm
I can sleep
with a firefly
companion
on my wall

The Blue Something

After another unsuccessful fishing trip
we were motoring back to the dock
when we spotted the blue something
caught in the weeds. It breeched
like the back of a baby whale,
closer we could see it was
a plastic barrel. It had been
in the water for a while,
there was a growth of slimy algae
and big mussel shells.
With no loop or handle to tie to
I got into the rowboat so
I could fight it to shore.
Slowly going, I managed
to roll it into the shallows.
Stamped on the side I could read
Envasa Plas SA, San Juan Argentina

but no mention of what it contained.
Of course I was hopeful for contraband.
Grandpa was worried it might be
filled with oil or something hazardous,
kicked off a ship. He was in favor of
leaving it alone, but I had to know.
Maybe it was part of a smuggling ring,
a radio antenna inside sending out
a weak signal even now.
I couldn't let it go—I could see
the headlines if I did—*New Jersey
Couple Discover Millions In Barrel!*
Or there could be the horror of
an informant's mangled body
crumpled up in there.
But 40 gallons of toxic mystery
almost won over, until I saw
the small hole in the top.
Now it seemed safe to find out
what it held inside. Argentina?
What did they export? What fell
overboard and drifted up the Atlantic
all the way here? What if after all
our empty fishing hours we caught
a drum full of pickled herring?
It was hard work to drag it onto
the rocky shore. Clear water
gushed from it. Grandpa got a hammer
and chisel and opened another hole
so the water poured out in a freshet,
not red, or stinking of gasoline,
or burning radioactivity bleaching
the shoreline. We let it all pour out
then I turned it, stood it upright and
looked through the little hole.

All blue lit inside, it held only
some water, a sprig of seaweed,
a bolt and a shard of plastic,
nothing else. Pulling it up
the wooden steps from the shore,
tied to a handline, across the grass
to the side of the shed, its drifting
journey has ended. It will make
the perfect rain barrel.

Floating Charlie

He lay flat
like a boat
on the Atlantic

drifting offshore
with the sun on him

quiet as an island

Oak Tree

Sleeping below the oak tree
all night rain and wind
acorns hitting the roof

Mirrors

Broken halves of seashells
mirrors filled with water
from the tide going out

Laundry

I tried fishing for the first time in years.
Tide was coming in, breezy blue water.
Casting, caught nothing but seaweed or eel grass
until finally the surface rippled as the hook was
breaking. A school of little mackerel followed it in
like laundry flapping around the line. I caught one
briefly but it was too small and fell off.

8 Year Old Egg

Humpty Dumpty fell off the swing.
There he sits, legs sticking out in front
his face flushed red, pouting with his hand
on his bumped head.

The Blue Lobster

Everyone wanted to get lobsters for supper
except for me, I was just along for the ride.
We got to the wharf and they took us
down to the end where they kept the pen
to show us the Blue Lobster. It was even
mentioned in the newspaper apparently.
We had not heard of it though. I mumbled
to my wife, maybe there was something
we could do to cheer it up. She laughed.
They keep it in its own cage like a prisoner.
Yes and here he is, taken out into daylight,
dripping water. The Blue Lobster is quite a
sight. Then they put it back and lock the lid.
Along the edges of the dock a school of those
little mackerel reappear, green and black
tiger stripes, they move like wind-up
submarines.

Just Before 6 A.M

Thick foggy morning
only white to see
sound of lobster boats
crows and waves
seagulls and terns
drops of rain on roof

Philadelphia to Akron

Flying at night
looking down at
all the lights
the deep swirls
carnivals, volcanoes
and city grids
as my daughter sleeps
on my shoulder

We're over countryside
where little roads blink
headlights turn
in the deep black
that stretches on
until I wonder
are we up or down
stars or the ground?

It's easy to imagine
another America
an inland ocean below
a forest a thousand miles wide
a Raymond Bradbury town
where a boy looks up
at the sound of a twinkling
rocket carrying us overhead

Cleveland Road

Lotus grow in the pond
beside the busy road
watching from the car
the air conditioner on
a white egret lands
sinking in flowers

The Same Radio

Open the window
the moon spins
like a record
Ohio music
crickets
a train
hurrying to
another town

6:30 A.M

On sand
where a heron
stood watching
the sun

The Vacant Lot

For as long as I've known it
filled with unmown grass and wild flowers
by now I guess you could call it a park

The Cricket Tide

At night
it returns
and we swim
in the sound

movement
made heavy
we get sleepy
and drown

Fox Subway

I hoped for a chance to see the fox.
Sometimes he appears running along
the narrow treed edge between
their yard and next door.
The neighborhood is linked
by a chain of thin green paths
a fox will follow. They must learn
these routes like subways…
go right at the beechnut
then quickly past the pool…
Even now, at 2 A.M
I might happen to hear
a rush of wind and see
the low orange blur go by.

Lummi Transit

It's a long way from the morning bike ride
to work. Usually I'll be looking at gardens
watching for glass in the road, knowing
I need air in the back tire and sometimes
it can't be predicted, the white van from
the Lummi reservation will appear.
Now I'm one week later, thinking of
that bus in this place, with a lot of land
in between us.

Giant Eagle

We stop next to a canoe
outside Giant Eagle
it's one of those Ohio
flash downpours
the parking lot is falling rain

By the time we get
the car doors open
the rain is done
water covers land
we step on lily pads
floating above the tar
the perch and carp
and silver grocery carts
stir below

A Factory Cloud

The heron left tracks
stamped into the sand
with iron precision

Where they stop
look up for
a factory cloud

                      On Quarry Road
                      the car just misses
                      a yellow butterfly

Michael

Michael sits
on the bench
outside Drug Mart
waiting
for a friend.
It's a small town
people cross
the hot tar
some of them
he knows.

37 Cent Lettuce

A few leafs
packaged
just enough
for a sandwich
wilted soft
and green as
a summer dress

Route 61

From a distance they look like crows
then something's not right, they're too big
and as the road passes the farmhouse, I see why.
There are three vultures perched on that roof.
One of them shuffles next to the chimney
like a bent old man in a hot overcoat.

Ohio Cloud Mountain

Going East
with Erie on the left

in all that flat
Cuyahoga Valley
the sky needs
something to build

a mountain
made of clouds

Edison Farm

They must have built the house in winter
and the snow got caught in it, leaving
the ghost of cold that never warmed
even in summer. The ruins were
a good place to stop after walking
in the hot open fields on the way
to town. The view out the window
stared down another mile before
the spires of the grain elevators
began.

Elyria

The sun goes down
the windmill is still
the flowers sleep
tilted at the moon

Screen windows
no thoughts
thunder far away

Ohio Buddha

In a garden
with hibiscus
Rose of Sharon
and birds

under the tree
eyes closed
with snails
upon his head

Watermelon

Surprised by a rabbit
in the backyard
eating seeds
under the birdfeeder.
Calm as a pond
it moves on
to the garden
tasting the sweet
fallen pink flowers.
When the sprinkler
starts it slips
into the green
suitcase of leaves
and is gone.

An Ordinary Sight

I spotted it go by
from the kitchen window
so we had to grab our bikes
and track it down on
the neighborhood blocks
Seneca Avenue, Mohawk Drive
left on Franklin to Winona Ave
finally catching the tall sight
as he came up Kiwanis
in the shade of elms.
He slowed and I asked him
what's it called that he rides.
"It's a High Wheeled Bicycle.
Back in the olden days they called it
an Ordinary Bicycle." Of course
because in those times it was
only an ordinary sight.

Goodwill

There were five boxes of Super 8 film reels.
My heroes, Charlie Chaplin, Laurel and Hardy.
I like to picture someone finding them
someone who comes along into the store
and sees them glowing there and knows
just what to do. In the cricket night
set up a projector, aim it at a garage
or a wide oak tree, make sure everyone's
around and let it roll.

Ohio Names

Mapped and
written down
not everything
is known

Unnamed
wet stones
jostle on
the beach

Air

Three bicycles in the garage
one of them has a flat tire.
I'll take the bike that doesn't
and ride it to the gas station
to see if they have an air pump.
It isn't far, under the cover of trees
then across the road and along the cracked
sidewalk. There's a lot of ironweed
growing beside the road, it fills the field.
Because of the name, I can't help thinking
those tall green stalks could be cut and
bound to make railroad tracks.
When I get there, past the gas pumps
on the corner where the road turns in
attached to a lamppost is the air compressor.
A metal box with a hose. It's free though
just press a button and air comes right out.

I ride back to the house, switch bicycles
and push the one with the flat tire
all the way to the gas station again.
Past the field, chicory and ironweed
with purple flower smokestacks
I feel a drop of rain.
From the way the clouds are
building and bruising together
it looks like one of those Great Lake
downpours will be happening soon.

Here's a detail I didn't notice
until I came back. The big sign
with the gas price on the road
says they also sell worms.

What if I ask about that?
It's probably an interesting story.
Are they grown locally?
How are they kept alive?
I guess that's what separates
this story from the Pulitzer Prize...
I'm only here for the air.

Cleveland Cloud

Fill that cloud
with Cleveland
and send it on

By the time
I get home
it will arrive
as rain

Acorns

This blanket
rain covering
began with
a few taps
like acorns
on the roof

Paper Airplane Dream

It's the crickets
and the ceiling fan
calm

time slowed down
to where a dream
comes easily

the day
all folded up
and flown
into night

4
FALL & WINTER

Back Home

A leopard slug
lifts its head
to greet me

Hum

On a window
in the barn
a bumblebee
so big
the glass hums

Reading Yasunari Kawabata
a three legged dog appears
and leans against me
tired. I pet its hot fur
then it hops away

The Tree Near Old Main

Its shadow is gone
the air is a vacancy
a haunted space
the birds avoid

What the Night Used to Be

When we first moved to this town
there was a Drive-In movie theater.
Also there used to be an airplane
flying around at night with lit up words
written in moving dots on the wings.
I can still picture it in the branches
of the willow tree. I can't remember
what it used to say but every time
I heard its slow hum, I would run
outside to read it goodbye.

Blackberry Ghost

picking blackberries
in the moonlight
thorns don't bother her

Deer Poem #1

Spied a deer
across the ditch
behind the branches
in someone's yard
just standing there

When they freeze
they go back
hundreds of years
You can almost
watch them disappear

Through this century
the walls we put up
the motorized age
our time is temporary

Further and further
the deer fade
to a place where
they know
we don't remember

Nothingness

Where the road valleys out
with the little pond on the right
and the cluster of houses on the left
there's a fog laying down like a blanket

I wonder if there's some bird
a stork or heron that gathers
the early morning mist and
twigs it together into a big nest

I was so intent walking in
trying to see if I could tell
when nothingness begins
where cars disappear
and people wander aimlessly

Deer Poem #2

Walking along
the museum of 7 AM
a deer painting
in the trees

Deer Poem #3

The second day
their yard is calm

In the corner
the deer waits for
houselights to go on

Deer Poem #4

Before I got there
I was thinking I'd like
to bring a present.
What would a deer want?
I could bring an apple
but they already have
their share off the trees.
Maybe a tangerine, or
some supermarket fruit
flown here from overseas?
One taste of that and
he would never forget.
For the rest of his life
that deer would be looking
for another pineapple.

Deer Poem #5

I told Rustle about the deer and asked,
"What do you think he's doing in their yard?"
as we passed that spot in our car.
Rustle said, "He's a spy deer.
He spies on whatever goes by."
Of course. I never considered
I'm not the only one watching.
He's wearing the slouch hat and raincoat
disguised, taking notes and melting back
into the forest to report on us.
As if to lend truth to this 6 year olds' theory
I haven't seen the deer since then
it seems that his cover is blown.

32nd & Seagull

Along 32nd Street
there's a little house
sometimes with a seagull
standing on the rooftop.
When it's there it makes noise
turning and shaking its wings out.
Sometimes another gull appears.
I only see these things if I'm out
walking the dog, or going to the store.
With the whole town to nest on,
it's odd for a bird to land there.
There's nothing about the place
to notice. Sometimes I forget
which house has the seagull on it.
One day as I walked past
a man was kneeling on the sidewalk.
He was digging dandelions.
I stopped and said hello.
He looked up and cupped his ear
as I asked, "What's the story with
that seagull on top of your house?"
He didn't mind telling me,
"It started showing up three years ago."
"Do you feed it anything?" I asked
picturing him throwing fish up there.
At my bus stop once I saw a woman
wearing a bright pink bathrobe
tossing bread on the roof of her house.
Seagulls and crows were perched
all around, waiting for her to leave.
"No," he said. "He just chose me."

Every September

Every September those prefab wooden stands
reappear in the parking lots of grocery stores
with names like *Windy's* or *Storm Shack* painted
on the side in circus colors. At a variety of prices
and sizes from a nickel thimble little puff of breeze
a child can toss, up to a carpet tube packed
with enough storm to take the green leaves
off a maple tree. And then for the next
few weeks the days and nights are spent
listening to people set them off
blowing away summer.

You Can't See a River
Only Its Water

This storm
is a river
rushing through
the air

Something So Important

Someone forgot to turn off the wind.
All night long it roared, creaked the house,
rattled the gate. There are things you should
know about your house, where the water
shut-off is, the fuse box. There are still things
about this house I'm discovering, like those old
cement stairs that appear out of the grass
underneath the lilacs. They don't go anywhere,
do they? They look like they used to walk
into a house that time has made invisible.
Or maybe someone left the wind on long ago
and the house blew away? Mysteries abound.
I didn't have time this morning to look around
for a lever or switch or whatever would do it,
I had to go to work. It looked like some furious
force had been corralled inside the front yard,
leaves and debris stirred up like a tidal pool.
And it went up, up, up to where seagulls
wheeled in the dim gray far above.
I was home by 4 o'clock. The wind
had tired, as it paced back and forth,
I could see the winter grass bend
beneath its pace. I went directly
to the barn and got the ladder.
It was time to put an end to this.
I leaned the ladder against the house
and climbed. I guess I had an idea
that's where I would find the valve
and sure enough, it only took a minute.
Just off the gable where the stanchion
for the TV aerial used to be, within
touching distance on the rough hide
of the fir tree there was a silvery,

rusting handle. I reached out and gave it
a good turn. That did it. The wind stopped,
all the tremor and shake of it died,
and it was quiet at last. I don't know
who puts something so important
so far away from where we can get it.

After The Wind

look how
the trees and flowers
leaves and petals
cover the ground

The Blackberry Creature

While the others ripened
plumped with juice
were plopped in buckets
in the summer sun
this one unpicked berry
glowers beneath a fuzz
of ghostly gray
Filled with a monstrous
knowing how short time is
this blackberry sticks
out of reach, dried hard
and withered in thorny vines

Charles Baudelaire

Caught on the thorn
at the height of the rose
he is torn
when I take him
off the vine

Words

like apples
waiting in the air

40 Watts of Apple

Unscrewed
from the branch
it's just right

carried back
to the house
a reading light

The Packard

I sell Packards.
You may have seen my lot
off the Mt. Baker highway.
I keep a few parked there
five or six in various stages
rust and slump, but still
good enough to catch your eye.
There are more for parts in back
some only skeletons
barely ideas of cars anymore.
The real prize I keep inside.
On pleasant starry nights
I turn off all the neon lights
and pull the clanking chains
to open the big garage door
not to see the view across the fields
or the big pyramid of mountain.
I turn my back to that.
I set my lawn chair on the gravel.
From there I look into the garage
at the blue lit spectacle
like a car pickled in a jar.
A 1949 Packard shiny and chrome
as a sea bass in the huge fish tank
I got from a bankrupt aquarium.
Preserved in embalming fluid
it will survive kept alive like that
for as long as the pharaohs in
the days of the Nile.

The Packard Migration

What I wasn't expecting
with the rainy season
and high waters was
the Packard migration.
Out in the field
the creek overflowed
and the Packard responded.
Its V-8 engine coughed
into life, wheels spun bubbles
its headlights like bright eyes
saw the way out and it went.
I didn't know about it
until the morning.
There was broken glass
and pools of water
and the tracks
easy to follow
in the tall damp weeds.

The Packard Hatchery

Now I've gone to great pains
to reverse the tide of history.
There's no reason to believe
that once again we can't see
thousands of Packards
on the roads of America.
What I started is a hatchery.
There are three cement pools
where they begin
little fingerlings
flickers of silver chrome
Packards no more than
a few inches long.
They school together
and drive in endless circles.
I care for them, make sure
they grow strong.
Of course it's a slow process
but eventually they will be released.
It's breathtaking to see it happen
when the waters of the last big tank
shimmer and out drives a new herd.
The Packards move cautiously at first
then picking up speed and really
making a run for it when their wheels
get the feel of the sunlit tar.

You're Right

There is a best way
to wash an apple
picked off the tree

hold it like a ball
roll it downhill
over the wet grass

Only Me

I noticed her spider web because it was a work of art
spun just above the height of my head. When I went
out the gate to the driveway I would miss it by only
an inch. She must have measured me and wove
that web with arithmetic. So I felt terrible
when I hit it one morning. I actually heard it snap
and felt the fiber wrap around my neck falling down.
I told her how sorry I was. She scurried along
the wall of the house pulling in armloads of silk.
But that wasn't the only time it happened.
Anywhere she put her web I'd be running into it
sooner or later, ruining her work. Feeling sorry
I bought a spool of thread and tried my best
to help her out, filling in a patch between
branches, well out of my way. I hung
the smallest yellow bells in the rigging
so I'd be sure to hear them ringing.
But a spider's success depends on
secrecy and invisibility, tying the air
up in knots you can't see is her strategy.
My bad designs and unwanted noise
wouldn't work to catch her meals.
The bugs knew better and flew
a different path, which left her
only me.

The Big Moth

By daylight
it's a white
plastic bag
caught in a tree

Cold Morning,
Pink & Blue Sky

I see her
every morning
walking to work
wearing the colors
of the sky

Spring Bird

You're too early
to fly this way
with covers
on our windows
to keep the cold
away

Sweet and
beautiful
singing bird
we miss you
and look for you
on our radios

We wait
for you
in our own
lonesome way
with a weight
on our heart

Winter Bee

Around my desk
in tired circles
a bee finds rest
on the plastic
ear of corn

pushing aside
the green silk
soft cloth
curling in there
to hibernate

He's done this before
slept through the cold
in a real autumn field
when there's some
last scent of honey
on the wind

The Cat With 9 Lives

Beside the house
a tall rose bush
a lilac and drainpipe
from the awning

A gray shadow
as Sammy jumps
passing over
the motorcycle
and flowerpots

The Scottish Horse

Russet fur parked
in a green field
slanting into
blue sky

The Little Pig's House

A silver trailer
filled with twigs
broken into pieces
brought to the dump

Mt. Baker View

After throwing away
a carload of trash
at the dump
turning on Slater Road
to go back home
there's the mountain
a cone of white snow
taller than everything

Beehive

The honeycomb
in the fireplace
keeps the house
warm and yellow

A Warm Blanket

left on the couch
a minute ago
when it poured
around you

The Great Speckled Bird

I was waiting for the bus
watching the sky blue morning
with a speckled pink and yellow cloud

We Live Below

a lid of clouds
bound to the tops of trees

we follow the crows
leading the way

calling out names
in the white

We All Have Places
Awaiting Our Arrival

Birds find
what they want
a branch
held like a hand
above the river

Bellingham Coal Train

I hear the cry
deep at night
after 3 A.M.
when I can't sleep
they roll that coal
in open car
after car
right through town
further upshore
to haul it away
to China

It must be the debt
for all our war
to have to dig
our own heart
out like that

How else can
the years of war
be accounted for
how else could we
collapse so far
every bullet, every filthy
hand to be greased
from here to there

That sound
brings up questions
How much is left?
How much more
can be hollowed out?
Where is it from?

How far do the tracks go?
Who are we fooling?
With these trains
tugging at
black veins

Yes, that's right
think of vampires
running dark at night
but also in the day
people will stop
drop their lives
to watch it
rumble through
their neighborhoods
until it's gone
eerie quiet
left after thunder

I've heard
people who live
close to the tracks
even with windows
closed tight
they still find
soot on the sills
on the cloth curtains
on their furniture
flitting in the air

We must be
deep in debt
I'm afraid
we must be
miles in the red

digging down
in pockets
finding no more
spare change
coming up with coal

1971 Ford

While we were eating
at the picnic table
surrounded by slides
and swings and fun

A policeman left
two yellow tickets
tucked beneath
your windshield wiper

Someday

growing in the woods
will be the dollar tree
and its leaves won't matter
fallen around on the ground
like a bank robbery

Sunny Meter

It's been 3 days
raining and windy
the front step is empty
no sign of Sunny
the neighbor's cat

Living In Water

We feel
every tremor
disturbing
the surface

When it's calm
we wonder
when it will
happen again

Chapter 10

Last night
watched the crows
crossing our yard
before dark

Bluebell the Mole

caught by the cat
left in the grass
time for a shovel
put it to rest

cut a piece of earth
lay the dead mole in

those big hands that
dug through the ground
now held out open
in surrender

cover him over
with a blanket of moss
and some bluebells
placed on top

The Barking Little Streetlight

There is nothing
you can hold onto
past this life
the only treasure
that matters
grows inside
your heart

Coyote Alarm Clock

At 4:30 AM
a coyote wakes me
carrying a box
full of lightbulbs
barefoot across
burning coals

Instant Coffee

A jar
filled with
a shadow

Chapter 14

Mornings
the whole town
flying in a white cloud

No wonder
we feel this way

Bellingham Bay, Saturday

I can only say it's beginning to read
like a horror movie script.
Saturday afternoon on a dock
in Bellingham Bay, a cold blue sky.
A dying stickleback is flipping over
in a pool of gasoline. It looks like
it's got a motor in it, taking it
to the next drop of spilled oil.
We don't stay long. I didn't expect
so much pollution. We're all just
riding out the storm. Even my son
tells me, when he falls on the lawn,
"I'm having a bad day." That's no lie.
I just wonder if we're in the middle,
or is the movie almost over?

The Floating Leaf

Sometimes
walking in the woods
you will see one
suspended in the air

It doesn't need a tree

Cabbage White

They tend to
the tops of fir trees
far out of reach.
Only once did I see
one close up
finding it dead
on the sidewalk.
It had the faint
pictures of crowns
on its wings.

The October bee
makes due with
dandelions

The Yellow Tree

half its leaves
have flown
onto ground

they are ducks
around a puddle
scattering in wind

6 Year Old Photographer

"That would have been
a perfect picture
if she was in it."

Daughter
On Orcas Island

You
could fly
a tall kite
so I can see
where you are

Japanese Breakfast

A bowl of rice
a book of haiku
suddenly
I'm late for the bus

Monday morning
a puddle is waiting
on the way to work

A wet dollar
painted on the street
unpeeling it

Driving over

chestnuts
popping
in the driveway

Winter Books

Each winter
becomes a book

Last year
sits on the shelf
frozen shut
cold and white

This year
the stories
fill with
wind and rain

Green Beans

eating from
a can of green beans
water running
off the fork

Lucy the Alligator

Around
folding chairs
we finally get
to pet her
surprised
how soft
like a moth
or a wave

The Third Morning

I remember
open the gate
carefully

it's okay

the spider web
is gone today

Rabbit Nightlight

On the trail
all I see
a white tail

A branch sways
an owl landed
in the gloom

Wet Morning

Finding
footprints
a cat
a dog
a man
walking
to where
he parked
his car
tires leaving
a dry square
on the tar

Morningtime Rhyme

The window is open
the shades are drawn
in a high-ceiling room
the lights are on

Recycle Day

That was Friday, two days ago when I got home
from work on the bus and saw our filled crates
still on the sidewalk. It was almost four o'clock.
After I got inside the house I called headquarters
to ask about the recycle pickup. "The truck is
running a little late," said the lady on the telephone.
We were eating when the blue truck showed up.
The brakes hissed as it stopped and a guy jumped
out to the sidewalk. He grabbed hold of the edge
of the shaggy lawn and gave it a sudden pull.
The house shook, everything became watery
and washed like a wave toward the recycle truck.
We were poured in with all the neighborhood
and hauled outside town. Now we just sit here.
I guess this used to be a field, everything
used to be something else.

The Nightwatchman

Something wakes me
each morning at 3
when I clock in.
Everyone is asleep
even the dog just lays there.
Nothing happens outside
but a passing car once
in a while. An hour
goes by, I toss and
turn and listen.
It might be raining
windy or utterly still.
The only thing I'm missing
is sleep.

Crowded Meadow

I've been in
this dream before
like a flower
waiting for
that one bee

Abigail

the blue flower
wears a paper mask
hides her looks
like Halloween

Sleeping Beauty

Of course she is
under a spell
cold and beautiful
Still
I can't help
thinking maybe
I am the one
to wake her

At the Bus Stop

Three girls
holding pumpkins
on their laps

October Is Wind

Push
pumpkins
before
the door

Their
orange light
will send
the cold wind
running

This Halloween

I knocked on our window
with a ghost on a stick
Rustle met me at the door
laughing, looking to see what
I held behind my back

Trick or Treating

When we go trick or treating our 8 year old son is dressed as an old fashioned reporter. He's wearing a rumpled suit and a hat with the word PRESS tipped into the band. A lot of the older people like the costume and even offer him two or three treats. After many Halloweens in this neighborhood I've come to know these houses—the ones that make an impression on me: where a little dog lives, a handmade path of stones, a talking head in a bubble, an old comedian and his wife, a castle, a haunted house, an ancient mansion where an old woman moves like a crane. Many of the houses are built with steep staircases or steps and some have amazing dark gardens. Where we begin happens to be one of my favorites. Up a tiled walkway made of concrete slabs, we are in his front yard. Every year the owner dresses this plot as a cemetery. There are joke names written on the headstones with props, a scarecrow and a few big spiders, a talking skull with red lit eyes, speakers playing some soundtrack of Halloween. Not far from his door the man will be standing, waiting for us with a flashlight and a big bowl of candy.

The Old House

It's been repainted
dark gray, not green anymore.
The lights are on as we go past
there's still a pumpkin on the steps.
Someone else lives there now.

Walking the dog
a cat hiding
behind a pumpkin

The Tuba Tree

turns into brass
then with a blast
all the leaves fall off

Raking Leaves Again

maple, alder
oak, poplar
and a red
soy sauce packet
someone dropped

Rumi's Book

Letting a few
drops of rain
land on the page

For Winter

flowers
plowed under
in chocolate rows

House in the Woods

Sunday walk
below the branches
a shower of rain
a squirrel
in the rafters
Further on
in another room
startling an owl
it flies deeper
into the leaves
the chimney beside
a green window sill

November
our house is caught
in a raindrop

Salmon Candles

Salmon are timing out
to the last sway
intent on the current
pointed upstream, knowing
the place they are going

their death shows
on fins and blotched
along their skin
white growing on them
in patches the way age
grows on us too

turned into ghosts
tossed out on the stones
along the curb of creek

even from a distance
up on the bluff
looking down the cliff
through the layers of trees
you can see the flow
the salmon shipwrecked
like pale yellow candles
waiting for nighttime
to glow in the dark

North Cascades

I have spent a lifetime
staring at mountains
and they have
kept me in view
whether I'm here
or miles away
it doesn't matter
they are
always there
to pin down
this table cloth
of travels

Car Turning Green

Three months parked
in one spot

That's all it takes
for moss to grow

On the Footbridge

We stop to watch
the slow floating creek
cold glass poured
over sand and
both of us
looking for fish

A white cat
licking ice
on the porch

The moon
shutting her door
only a sliver of light

The Return of
the Blue Plastic Swimming Pool

The sky before
the sun climbs out
a white full moon
and a hundred crows
thrown like a net
overhead

Beside the leaning
wooden fence
the blue plastic
swimming pool returns
crouching its hoop
over the frozen
white toothed
unbent grass

That Christmas Tree

At 7 AM
there's snow
powdering the hills
and she is taking
her tree for a walk

That's what I thought
but she tossed it
in the gully
next to the pond
believing
no one would see
on this dim lit morning

But she was wrong
now two people
from time to time
will glance at
that thrown out
Christmas Tree

Coffee Machine

A paper cup
falls down
and fills

Milk White Sky
Flecked With Birds

A cat sitting
in the window
like a pitcher
you could pour
into a bowl

Prettier Than a Bird

How can she
be so pretty
so early
this morning?
Seeing her
I've forgotten
the bird
who woke me

School Bus

A hurried kiss
"I love you"
up the stairs
he goes

I step back
as the bus leaves
to see my son
his little shape
going where a girl
sleeps in the window

That Summer Song

This morning a robin
watched me on the path

I gave that summer song
they sing on lawns
when it's warm

A joke though
it's still February
snow on the way

The robin chirped twice
and gave me a look
but when I got through
the forest to the hill
on the other side
I could hear that
summer song
repeated

We Are

Oh sure
we are
sailing along
happily

our house
a little
wooden ship
in the cold

and out
the chimney
smoke pours
dreamily

The Peach Can

filled with
three day's ice
riding in it

overnight
it turns to water
winter nearly done

Warm Sun

Listening
ice is melting
off the white
alder trees

tapping onto
blackberry leaves

PLAYGROUND

1: SPRING & SUMMER

Soft Rain
Rainy Morning
The Cow Ghost
The Plastic-Coated Cat
The Willow Orchard, Part 1
The River Lover
Spring Ladder
The Float
Stuck in the Air
On the Beautiful Planet
Worm Salvage Work
Everything Thrown Out in the Rain
Basho, the Japanese Poet
The Gray Street Cherries
Weather Trade
The Chestnut
Silkworms
Green & Yellow
Outside
Little Soul
Neighborhood Stories
In Other Words
Don't Forget the
Mountain Flowers
Settled In
Tuned To Water
No Snow This Year
The Rhododendron Seller
The Beehive Recital

Spindled Out
A Glass of Wind
The Curve
Sleep
The Extra Day
Petals
Walking with a Flower
The Hidden Place
Whistling Apricot
Apricot Music
June Weather
Umbrella
Library Spider
Red Leaf
Rhododendron
Speckled Dog
Lawn Mower
Swallowtail
The Bumbling Bee
The Bird Planet
A Family of Deer
The Underwater Dog
One Morning Instead
The Dragonfly Driver
The Shepherd from Iran
DC-3 Be Gone
Another Ferris Wheel
The Nightbird
Satori
Going To Ohio
Almost a Cardinal
Ohio Garden
Holy Water
Praying Mantis
Heron Doing Time

Above the Field
Sundown
The Bed
Green Yarn
Limpets
Out of the Plant
Away From Work
Climate Control
Anymore
The Marx Birds
For Louie
Playground
Lady Day
Free Kittens
Clockwork Rabbit
Ring Chimes
Lake Erie
Welcomes
3 Elephants in Cleveland
T.C.M.B.C
Cleveland Block
Laundry Chutes
Cleveland Disappears
Perry Como Pure Gold
A Whale
The Hummingbird
Salting
Even If
Last Day
Pictures & Words
Slow Bicycles
Ohio Pull
Old Sights

2: FALL & WINTER

Returning
To Sweeten
Blackberry Family Portrait
The Good Morning
Morning Bike Ride
Yellow Apple
Racing a Bee
Summer's End
Sitting Outside
After Summer
The Sunny House
Summer Things
The Red Wagon
Monday Morning
Tilling the Soil
The Eyes of Animals
One Crow
Stopped like a Balloon
Fog So Thick
The Foghorn Calls for Them
A Code
Barns
Cow
Blackberry Player Piano
Raking Leaves
Put Down the Rake
Chestnut Tree
The Fall Car
Bird Shaped Leaf
Varied Thrush
Clouds Surround an Orange Moon
Ray
The Good Couch

Cold Wet Dog
Summer is Gone
Umbrella Story
Love Again
I Have Imagined and Now We Are Real
19th Century Bird
The Panda Bears
Thursday Morning
The Word Tree
Only
This Hand
Halo
Waiting for Sleep
At 2 A.M
The Highway Surf
Walking the Dog Story
Video
The Wishing Well Custodian
Big Ideas
Everything is Going Somewhere
Mr. & Mrs. Soft and Warm
Walking in the Snow
Pink Mountain
Winter Apples
Porcelain
A Loom in the Snow
The Five Year Old Land
2:50 A.M.
Song of the Tin Man
The Creature
The Sawhorse
Bus Sound
Unwinding
Some Days
Winter Trees

Watching Crows
The Hula Hoop Hero
Directions Folded to a Bird's Wing
Spent Time

3: SPRING & SUMMER

Morning, Bus Stop
Under Water On The Lawn
International Orange
March Morning
A Broom
Two Rabbits
Two Spiders
A Cranefly
The Willow Orchard, Part 2
Sending Out Thoughts
Early Summer Swallow
A Bird Shaped Kite
Mermaid Laundry
Add Water
April Dream
Woken By
All The Puddlefish
The Lotus Pond
Mr. Thank You's Cloud
Sunday Nap
The Plum Map
Shortcut
Paul
Daisies
Breasts
Parking Lot Bouquet
Quiet
Larry

Rain
Bugs
Dave
Breeze
Telephone Poles
Mt. Baker
The Tooth Fairy
Paint
Prayer
Jason's Barn
Nooksack River
32nd Street
Bird Taxi
Bird Taxi Purr
Bird Taxi Mystery
Bird Taxi Times
Bird Taxi Boy
Bird Taxi Rain
Bird Taxi Bicycle
Bird Taxi East
Bird Taxi Me
Bird Taxi Belief
Today
Park
The Forgetting Birds
The Silkworm
Furniture in the Woods
A Plastic Chair
P'ang Yun
Landmark
A Borrowed Bird
Pearl Street
Paperback Crop
Tomatoes for Sale
Humpty Dumpty

Franklin Construction
Who Wouldn't Want A Gorilla Mask?
The Ohio Window
Two Cantaloupes
The First Morning Chore
On A River In Ohio
Satch
Two Mourning Doves
The Ohio Wheel
Hydrangea Legs
Marlene Dietrich
After a Dream
A House in Maine
Red Rose
Cuba
Gene's Beagle
The Lobster Wars
The Blue Path
The Biggest Fish
Watermelon Fishing
The Luna Moth
Rachel's House
A Yard Sale
Short Wave Radio
Summer Reading
King Medicine
Noah Road
Seagull
Tree Cup
Alice on the Seashore
Lighthouse
The Blue Something
Floating Charlie
Oak Tree
Mirrors

Laundry
8 Year Old Egg
The Blue Lobster
Just Before 6 A.M.
Philadelphia to Akron
Cleveland Road
The Same Radio
6:30 A.M
The Vacant Lot
The Cricket Tide
Fox Subway
Lummi Transit
Giant Eagle
A Factory Cloud
On Quarry Road
Michael
37 Cent Lettuce
Route 61
Ohio Cloud Mountain
Edison Farm
Elyria
Screen Windows
Ohio Buddha
Watermelon
An Ordinary Sight
Goodwill
Ohio Names
Air
Cleveland Cloud
Acorns
Paper Airplane Dream

4: FALL & WINTER

Back Home
Hum
Reading Yasunari Kawabata
The Tree Near Old Main
What the Night Used to Be
Blackberry Ghost
Deer Poem #1
Nothingness
Deer Poem #2
Deer Poem #3
Deer Poem #4
Deer Poem #5
32nd & Seagull
Every September
You Can't See A River, Only Its Water
Something So Important
After The Wind
The Blackberry Creature
Charles Baudelaire
Words
40 Watts of Apple
The Packard
The Packard Migration
The Packard Hatchery
You're Right
Only Me
The Big Moth
Cold Morning, Pink & Blue Sky
Spring Bird
A Winter Bee
The Cat With 9 Lives
The Scottish Horse
The Little Pig's House

Mt. Baker View
Beehive
A Warm Blanket
The Great Speckled Bird
We Live Below
We All Have Places Awaiting Our Arrival
Bellingham Coal Train
1971 Ford
Someday
Sunny Meter
Living In Water
Chapter 10
Bluebell the Mole
The Barking Little Streetlight
Coyote Alarm Clock
Instant Coffee
Chapter 14
Bellingham Bay, Saturday
The Floating Leaf
Cabbage White
The October Bee
The Yellow Tree
6 Year Old Photographer
Daughter on Orcas Island
Japanese Breakfast
Monday Morning
A Wet Dollar
Driving over
Winter Books
Green Beans
Lucy the Alligator
The Third Morning
Rabbit Nightlight
A Branch Sways
Wet Morning

Morningtime Rhyme
Recycle Day
The Nightwatchman
Crowded Meadow
Abigail
Sleeping Beauty
At the Bus Stop
October Is Wind
This Halloween
Trick or Treating
The Old House
Walking the Dog
The Tuba Tree
Raking Leaves Again
Rumi's Book
For Winter
House in the Woods
November
Salmon Candles
North Cascades
Car Turning Green
On the Footbridge
A White Cat
The Moon
The Return of the
     Blue Plastic Swimming Pool
That Christmas Tree
Coffee Machine
Milk White Sky Flecked With Birds
Prettier Than a Bird
School Bus
That Summer Song
We Are
The Peach Can
Warm Sun

Allen Frost reading from *Playground* manuscript in backyard, May 14, 2014. Photo by Rustle Frost.

These poems are collected from self-published
chapbooks written 2007—2013:
*Ohio Time, Bird Taxi, Radio, A Reversed Cat,
The Yellow Tree, Animals Ghosts and Outer Space,
Signals, Not to Worry, Ohio Silver Mine, 14 Animals,
Travel, 33 Landmarks, The Peaceful Island, Praises*

"Lady Day" published in *Labyrinth*, 2009
"The Extra Day" published in *Inkspeak*, 2011
"Bellingham Coal Train" published in *Clover*, 2012

Other Books by the Author

Ohio Trio (Bottom Dog Press 2001)

Bowl of Water (Bottom Dog Press 2003)

Another Life (Bird Dog Publishing 2007)

Home Recordings (Bird Dog Publishing 2009)

The Mermaid Translation (Bird Dog Publishing 2010)

The Selected Correspondence of Kenneth Patchen
       edited by Allen Frost (Bottom Dog Press 2012)

The Wonderful Stupid Man (Bird Dog Publishing 2012)

Saint Lemonade (Good Deed Rain 2014)

www.ingramcontent.com/pod-product-compliance
Lightning Source LLC
Chambersburg PA
CBHW020400080526
44584CB00014B/1112